T0248951

Daniel Ward

THE CANARY AND THE CROW

OBERON BOOKS
LONDON

WWW.OBERONBOOKS.COM

First published in 2019 by Oberon Books Ltd
521 Caledonian Road, London N7 9RH
Tel: +44 (0) 20 7607 3637 / Fax: +44 (0) 20 7607 3629
e-mail: info@oberonbooks.com
www.oberonbooks.com

Copyright © Daniel Ward, 2019

Daniel Ward is hereby identified as author of this play in accordance with
section 77 of the Copyright, Designs and Patents Act 1988. The authors
have asserted their moral rights.

All rights whatsoever in this play are strictly reserved and application for
professional performance should be made to Daniel Ward c/o Oberon
Books, 521 Caledonian Road, London N7 9RH (info@oberonbooks.com)
and for amateur performances to Oberon Books. No performance may
be given unless a licence has been obtained, and no alterations may be
made in the title or the text of the play without the author's prior written
consent.

You may not copy, store, distribute, transmit, reproduce or otherwise make available this publication (or any part of it) in any form, or
binding or by any means (print, electronic, digital, optical, mechanical,
photocopying, recording or otherwise), without the prior written
permission of the publisher.

A catalogue record for this book is available from the British Library.

PB ISBN: 9781786827975
E ISBN: 9781786827968

Cover image by Josh Moore

Typeset by Antares Publishing Services Pvt Ltd

Visit www.oberonbooks.com to read more about all our books and to buy them. You will
also find features, author interviews and news of any author events, and you can sign up for
e-newsletters so that you're always first to hear about our new releases.

10 9 8 7 6 5 4 3 2 1

Characters

THE BIRD
Daniel Ward

THE CAGE / SCHOOLKID 2 / MATHS TEACHER
/ KEYBOARD WARRIOR 1 / JAMES /
THE CANARY
Rachel Barnes

THE CAGE / BIG YEAR 9 / SCHOOLKID 1 /
KEYBOARD WARRIOR 2 / ALEX / RICHARD /
HEAD OF YEAR
Laurie Jamieson

THE CAGE / SNIPES
Nigel Taylor

The Actor exists outside of the linear story and should be performed as simply and as conversationally as possible.

This is a gig theatre piece that works like a concept album. The linear story acts as the "tracks" for the piece, broken down into acts and scenes, however between these "tracks" THE BIRD has the freedom to talk to the audience and interact as they choose. These interactions are adlibbed and it's the choice of the ensemble as to when and how often they occur. THE BIRD is the lead singer, however at different points others from the band (THE CAGE) may come forward to take the lead for a given "track" and adopt the role of THE BIRD.

The tracks are different to the lessons. The lessons follow subjects from the GCSE reforms up to 2020 that have been enforced to create a more demanding curriculum.

The lessons inform the tracks via poetry, terminology or artistically in some other way.

All named roles are to be played by THE BIRD/CAGE.

THE CAGE acts much like chorus. They can inform a scene at any point through music, text or otherwise. THE CAGE can act individually or have a group dynamic.

THE CAGE has no fixed number of members.

All song lyrics have the freedom to be rewritten by THE BIRD and THE CAGE depending on the sound that they have deemed fit for that track.

Italic, centered text indicates text sung or rapped or otherwise performed.

/   Indicates an interruption

&&   Indicates a Musical interlude or cue.

As the audience enter the space the hype man gets the audience ready, making it clear that this is a rave that needs them in order to exist. THE BIRD and THE CAGE also have the freedom to adlib and interact with the Audience as they please.

Prologue

THE ACTOR

We are at drama school and often people come to talk to us. Alumni, directors, creatives, whoever. This time a famous black actor has come to talk to us, which is nothing that unusual, except this time the actor only wants to talk to the BAME students. Cue a swath of emotions from every white student. Outrage about being excluded. Suspicion at what those sneaky blacks were planning. Everyone had something to say. The incident became known as Black Attack, which speaks for itself.

Anyway, the famous black actor's wish is granted and the few black students that are training are given a room to wait in. We, the black students, are curious as well, because after all we don't know what's going on either.

The actor comes in. Sits down, is amiable, cool, everything is vibes and then the question comes.

How is it being black at drama school?

A simple question but it is followed by quite a long pause.

No one really knows how to answer.

It turns out the famous black actor is worried. A friend of theirs, another famous BAME actor has recently had something of a breakdown. This breakdown has stemmed from their treatment and training at drama school, decades before. The actor in question had the breakdown because of an identity crisis. The person that they had come into drama school as wasn't the same as the person that they had left drama school as. The actor in question had left behind their cultural identity to succeed in an industry dominated by posh white people. The actor had become an "acceptable black" and this had resulted in a breakdown a long time later.

The famous black actor had come because they didn't want the same thing to happen to us.

They wanted to know if the same kind of cultural whitewashing was still happening.

I never answered then but I'll answer now

Growing up as a black boy or girl you learn about who people and society expect you to be.

These are the lessons I learned.

Taking it all the way back.

Ten years old in my front room.

THE CAGE starts playing music. During the following the Actor becomes THE BIRD.

The Bird.

&&

TRACK ONE – THE DROP

<u>*Chorus*</u>
A letter through the letterbox
Carries weight, carries power

THE BIRD: A letter through a letterbox. Hits the floor, it means nothing to me, but everything to her. Her is Mum. Single mother, only child. The letter comes. We are black. The letter comes and I can feel the weight. The letter carries weight. The letter carries power, but I don't understand why. I just know she, mum, is afraid to open it. Looks at me,

THE CAGE: You open it.

THE BIRD: Mum is fearless, so why is she afraid?

THE CAGE: She is the cat's mother.

THE BIRD: I don't understand, but I don't want to open it. Whatever is in that letter, it's causing my mum to panic and that panics me, so I say – I don't want to open it. She-/ Mum- she,

THE CAGE: / She is the cat's /mother.

THE BIRD: / She is the cat's mother. Mum. Mum snatches the letter out of my hand. Opens it. Rips it open.

And Mum screams. I have heard screaming before, but not like this. This is different. This is an unfamiliar scream. This is happy. A happy scream? Screaming with joy and jumping up and down. So, I jump up and down and then I start screaming and we are both screaming jumping up and down and it's fun, so I go along with it, but I still don't know why...

THE CAGE: You got in! You got in!

THE BIRD: OK.

&&

THE BIRD goes for a walk.

THE BIRD: OK. Nice day. Time to roll. Time to play. What you say? What you saying?

THE BIRD greets THE CAGE.

Got me gassed. Super Saiyan. Only one place to go.

THE CAGE: Wagwan, Wah blow?

THE CAGE greets THE BIRD.

THE BIRD: Dun know.

THE CAGE: Dun know!

THE BIRD & THE CAGE: To the park.

&&

TRACK TWO – RAINBOW CROW

<u>*Chorus*</u>
Trees Leaves Bushes Weed
Tress Leaves Bushes Weed

THE BIRD: The park is the place that we go. There is no green in this park, but we go.

There is no green in this park, no trees, no leaves, no bushes in this park, but we go.

We are young, so they call us Youngers.

They are old, so we call them Olders.

There is green is this park, so they go. There is green in this park,

Trees…

Leaves …

Bushes…

Weed.

In this park, so they go.

It's our place, a metal cage – four sides – one you should never stand in because people piss there, one I don't like standing in because girls get fingered there, but it is ours. A metal cage of freedom. Our birdcage. This is where we jam, play music, kick ball and chill and it has been that way forever. For my forever, as I'm only ten so it's all I've known, but I know it existed before me. Maybe not a park, but it has been there forever.

Cavemen had a spot like this, maybe even Jesus.

Today is a day like any other, except I am hyped. Just running around skinning teeth.

SNIPES: Rah, are you on something lil man?

THE BIRD: It's Snipes. Ryan to you. Snipes to me. You can only call him Snipes if you are cool with him. His mum calls him Snipes but you, you would have to call him Ryan.

Snipes is fifteen, but he is old. Not just an Older, fully old. He feels like he comes with a mortgage.

> What must you have seen,
> To be that old at fifteen.

I say the same thing that had been bouncing around in my head all day.

THE BIRD: I got in!

SNIPES: That's good man, got in where?

&&

THE BIRD: And I stop, because this is the first time someone has asked me. Everybody, *everybody* already knows my mum had been chatting so much. I have spoken to about ten people today who've said;

THE CAGE: Congratulations!

Such good news!

Well done!

Great job!

THE BIRD: People I don't know. Strangers on the street. I almost feel like saying

What, my mum hasn't told you yet?

But I don't.
Instead,
I just say,
Patrician Boys.

SNIPES: That's serious, is that you yeah? That's a private school init? You're blessed.

THE BIRD: Yeah, on a scholarship had to pass a test.

SNIPES: That's BIG man. Good look.

THE BIRD: And there is nothing but love. And I can't stop smiling because today I am a king.

Ok. Nice day.

THE CAGE: Time to roll. Time to play.

THE BIRD: What you say?

THE CAGE: What you saying?

THE BIRD: Got me gassed.

THE CAGE: Super Saiyan.

THE BIRD: Only one place to go.

THE CAGE: Wagwan, Wah blow?

THE CAGE greets the audience.

THE BIRD: Dun know.

THE CAGE: Dun know!

THE BIRD & THE CAGE: Back Home.

&&

TRACK THREE – A NUMBERS GAME

Chorus
Options options
Which one do you like?
Options options
Like I really have an option

THE BIRD: New tings to know. New things to see.

The lessons start pouring in like a stream.

Learning about life as I start down this path.

First Lesson.

Always.

THE BIRD & THE CAGE: Maths.

For the maths lesson there is a numbers game, which can be interpreted dramatically as the company see fit.

THE BIRD: I got into four (*four*). By the fourth it's routine, no screams but just an acknowledgement.

Happy but expected.

Then I look at these schools and I don't like them. My mum's considering options, options,

"Which one do you like?"

Like I really have an option.

But really, to me, I have to say,

Fully,

None! (*zero*)

They're all the same. No difference.

I know I have to pick one but our priorities are…

Different.

My mum is talking about

THE CAGE: League tables and UCAS

THE BIRD: And I'm thinking you are overlooking the key facts.

&&

Why are there no girls?

Why are there no girls?

Why are there no girls?

THE BIRD: Every single one; all boys.

Every.

Single.

One. (*One*)

Don't get me wrong I'm not thinking about a future with girls like *that,* I'm ten (*ten*), but I've grown up with them and they've been a part of my life since day, so I find myself asking why?

It just doesn't make sense.

Also, don't get me wrong I've had girlfriends before, when I was five (*five*) I had six (*six*). More girlfriends than my actual age, ya get me.

That's my first beef. This is my second (*two*).

And the biggest.

The girl's thing is peak, but it doesn't bother me as much as this.

I keep hearing the same thing consistently;

&&

THE CAGE: We are not a football school. We play rugby. We play RUGGER!

We are not a football school, we play rugby. We play RUGGER!

We are not a football school. We play rugby. We play RUGGER!

&&

THE BIRD: I'm sorry, where are we? I thought this was England not New Zealand.

I'm black not all black, don't give me that crap.

Never in my life has rugby even been a thing.

Every day we play FOOTBALL

We watch FOOTBALL

We speak about FOOTBALL.

I am fully in FOOTBALL

I've got football pyjamas, football bedsheets the whole nine (*nine*) yards and they're trying to take that away from me? On top of that in an *all-boys* school?

What do we talk about?

Who is going to be playing rugger at lunch?

Not me.

Never me.

There are other things that bother me, minor beef.

Ties and regulation backpacks,

Latin mottos, I can deal with all that,

15

But no football?

And that becomes the deciding factor. The major thing for me going into year seven (*seven*) is that Patrician Boys has a Powerleague.

An actual Powerleague attached to the school.

Eight (*eight*) astro-turf pitches that I can play on every single day.

For free. (*Three*)

Nuts.

My mum deals with stuff I don't care about, like entry to Russell Group universities but when we come together it's the only choice. Luckily for me it's in the top ten (*ten*) in the country, so she can't say nothing.

I end up going there.

TRACK FOUR – ONE SIDED HISTORY

Chorus
First day
Takes the piss
Let's go back
It went like this

THE CAGE: Second Lesson.

History.

THE BIRD: First day I get into a fight and my mum gets called in.

First day.

Takes the piss.

How does it happen in the first place? *Let's go back.*

&&

It went like this.

I'm running around as you do in a break when you are eleven, and I bump into a kid, knock over his coke and it falls on the floor. This kid is big. Year Nine. I'm Year Seven, he looked at me, I looked at him and before I could apologise, he said:

BIG YEAR 9: *(Looking up and down with disgust.)* Are you going to buy that back?

You *better* buy that back.

THE BIRD: And I'm like *(slowly turning head)* … Rah. I know that what he's saying is personal. That if anyone else had knocked over his coke he'd probably say "no worries man" and get on with his day but because it's me, he's reacting differently. He looks at me and I look at him and despite what he's saying, I know what he *means*.

So, I fight him.

Even with this on a different day, I probably would've reacted better maybe laughed it off, but before this exchange I'm already a bit sensitive, a bit on edge.

Why?

Let's go back.

&&

First day of high school is a big deal, right? Huge.

But in my family and with my mother that is multiplied.

It's a statement of success. She cried and cried.

When you are a single parent living in an area outside "catchment" zones,

That isn't particularly known,

For anything positive

And your son gets into one of the best schools in the country.

On a scholarship!

Boy, the pride, the pride!

She, is prouder of me,

Than she has ever been,

I walk into that classroom with her pride emanating from me.

My head held high.

And you know my mum made sure I was on point. New everything, new trousers, new shoes, new haircut – new national backpack association approved backpack (thing is disgusting.)

I walk into class ready to take over the world!

&&

And I meet my new classmates and it's cool and everything, but something is off. Somehow people seem a bit weird, like maybe a bit scared of me. It could just be the environment, new school and people are nervous; however, it doesn't feel like it. It feels like it's me.

I know in this moment, people, or at least some people in this class, view me as different.

As other.

Nothing major but an unshakeable sense of other nonetheless.

Now, this is a feeling that black people become accustomed to. A feeling that becomes familiar over the years but today it's new, and I don't like it. A woman walking into a new workplace surrounded by men might know this feeling. Maybe.

There are thirty-one kids in my class and two of us are black. Five are Asian and the rest are white. We're the only black guys in the whole year, so they put the two of us together like, here you go make friends with each other little black boys, but whatever. But even the other black boy isn't

Quite.

Like.

Me.

He fits in better. Or at least people seem to warm to him easier. No one is rude, there's no drama, but the feeling of other is planted. In every interaction I can feel there's a half beat, a wink. Something where somebody checks themselves,

But I can tell they,

Want to say . . .

Something.

Fast forward.

&&

I bump into a kid, he looks at me I look at him and before I can apologise he says:

Silence

Without saying it, he says:

THE CAGE: What are you doing here? Is this some kind of mistake? You don't belong here.

THE BIRD: What are you doing here? Is this some kind of mistake? You don't belong here

And in this moment, he doesn't just insult me, but my pride.

And my mother's pride.

And I don't like it.

So I fight him.

Fast forward.

&&

Sitting in my Head of Year's office. My mum is in the office, sitting down next to me and they're going through my file.

HEAD OF YEAR: This permanent record is the size I would expect a sixth former's to be. This, in its own way is quite incredible but young man unless you change your ways you will be going nowhere in a hurry, do you understand? Now I have been told this attack was unprovoked is that true?

Well?

THE BIRD: Yes.

HEAD OF YEAR: Well, at least you're honest.

I'm afraid I have no choice but to gate you. You'll be outside my office for every lunch and break for a week. You must do better. There are many people who wanted a place here, you must remember how lucky you are. There are many who would have given an arm and a leg for that scholarship. This school is a privilege, and at any time it could be taken away. Remember that.

&&

THE BIRD: My mum is not speaking but I can feel her. Her pride and her hope has changed into something else. I can feel her fear. I can feel her anger. After all she / Mum she…

THE CAGE: / She is the cat's mother.

THE BIRD: She… /Mum. Mum has just heard that her son attacked someone unprovoked and I can feel her looking into the future and seeing terrible things. Seeing brutality. Seeing violence. Seeing murder. Seeing an out of control kid with real anger problems, destined to be another black statistic, to be dead or in prison. Mum is afraid. But I can't even tell her it's not like that because I can't even explain it myself. It's the first time I've experienced something like that. Politics. Well I can't explain it yet. It's only years later I'll realise that I could have told her. That my experience wasn't particularly unique, and she could've told me many stories just like it herself. But I don't, so when I got home I just get licks.

&&

THE CAGE: Lesson Three, Politics

THE BIRD:

It's not what you think trust it's not,
But man can't think on the spot,
Trust when I say what I got,
In my heart is the truth, it's a lot, it's a lot, it's a lot
But I can't get it out,
Head screaming doubt,
Like it is what it is, but it's not.

21

It's deeper than that,
My head's full of facts,
But you won't get it,
So I can't say that

I know you don't see what I see,
You don't understand what I speak
Our eyes see things differently,

I know what my version is
But to you my facts are alternative,
We in the same place at the same time
But two worlds.
Politics.

How can I know,
Which way to go,
Which way to stand,
Which way to roll,
Which way to back up,
When you say BACK UP!
Tryna get my back up,
With my man's back up,
To the wall,
Like a moot,
Like a tool,
Like you can rub my first in the dirt,
Why must I stop, whilst you search
For due cause to give,
Bored of this,
Bare blue light, so Lord is this
All there is,
Please let there be more than this,
Take the piss,
Here trying to live,
But if I died,

Would you give a shit?

Would you really give a shit?

POLITICS

I know you don't see what I see,
You don't understand what I speak,
Our eyes see things differently,

I know what my version is,
But to you my facts are alternative,
We in the same place at the same time,
But two worlds.
Politics

Does it even matter, who's in control?
When the fires starts, we already know,
Ain't no one here for our souls,
Cept the ones already in the hole,
The ones who the heat already reaches,
Can't be silenced, never speechless,
Will fight for what RIGHT teaches,
Well dem man LEFT on the beaches,
Bunnin up, to improve their features,
While people bun to helpless screeches,
And you really wanna ask what the beef is?
And you really don't know what the beef is?

Coz it's not personal,
With me it's a person who'll
Never see the earth and all,
Their talent has gone to waste,
Their struggle has been replaced,
With a man who's just here for gain,
Don't really care about the pain,
Coz when the greatest need was there to be taken,
That's when you found out you were most forsaken,

That's why I call you a Paigon, Paigon!
Paigon
Paigon
POLITICS

I know you don't see what I see,
You don't understand what I speak
Our eyes see things differently,

I know what my version is
But to you my facts are alternative
We in the same place at the same time
But two worlds.
Politics.

TRACK FIVE – FIX UP

Chorus
Trees Leaves Bushes Weed
Trees Leaves Bushes Weed

THE CAGE: Only one place to go.

THE BIRD: Dun know.

THE CAGE: Dun know.

THE BIRD & THE CAGE: To the park.

SNIPES: What's good man, what you saying?

THE BIRD: Nothing.

SNIPES: How you getting on at the school?

THE BIRD: Not good, got into a fight.

SNIPES: Already? Why?

THE BIRD: No reason.

SNIPES: I understand. Sometimes you just got to fight.

THE BIRD: And I join him in the park doing nothing. Because there is nothing to do. Except sit.

SNIPES: This is dead.

THE BIRD: But slyly I know he's lying. Because when you sit in a park doing nothing, trust me there's nothing you rather be doing.

SNIPES: You shouldn't fight ya na. You're smart, don't need to get caught up in bullshit like me. Next year I'm looking to leave this whole situation. M-Town's too small for me. I'm on money and movements. Straight, ambition fam, trust me. Whips, gal, P. For real though fam, you got a bright future don't fuck it up.

&&

THE BIRD: And we sit.

And we sit.

And we sit.

And it's fucking great.

So, I fix up. Or try to.

Not because of what Snipes said, that's stuff I already knew.

But because it's time.

Time.

New school, new start, new me.

&&

Lessons are good. But tough.

Maths. History. Politics.

They make everyone learn a poem to read to the class.

25

This is mine.

The Canary and the Crow

Together were two cages hung,
For music and for show;
In one a fine canary sung,
In t'other screech'd a crow.
One charm'd the household with his song,
The other vex'd it with his cries;
Forever cawing all day long,
He call'd for bread, and cakes, and pies.

And people fed him to his fill,
As the best way to keep him still.
Loud rang the sweet canary's strain,
He ask'd for naught, and sung in vain.
For none supplied his pressing needs,
Or gave him water, or his seeds.

Those most delighted by his chants,
Were quite oblivious of his wants.
They liked him well enough, 'twas true,
But never gave him what was due.
At last one day they found him dead,
Merely for want of being fed.
"Alas!" folks cried, "how can we spare
A songster so beyond compare!
How could he die?—a bird so rare!"

But while they thus express surprise,
The crow keeps up his stunning cries,
And still is fed on cakes and pies.

TRACK SIX – JOURNEYS

Chorus
Morley's, Betfred, Yoga, Pilates
One long road and the whole world changes

THE CAGE: Lesson Four, Geography (human, cultural and a bit of physical).

THE BIRD: This bus journey is something else. *Long.* It's been months and I'm still not used to it. I've never got a bus more than ten minutes before and this is over an hour. It's mad though. The world changes. It starts off with Morley's and Betfred and ends in yoga, pilates and dog groomers.

Some things are the same. There is a Greggs and a newsagents both places. Charity shops as well. But the charity shops at the end have sales, which makes no sense to me.

&&

My class is calm. I've made friends, Richard, James. They are cool, everyone is. Everything's kinda settled down.

I find myself going between two worlds. Chilling with school friends during the day and chilling with guys I grew up with at night.

They are different but weirdly similar and both fascinated by each other,
always asking questions
and I've became the oracle.

&&

SCHOOLKID 1: What are rude boys like?

THE BIRD: Kind of like you, I guess.

SNIPES: Fam, do any of them have horses?

THE BIRD: Yeah, some of them have horses.

SNIPES: Fuck, they really have horses?

THE BIRD: Yeah some, some of them have horses!

SCHOOLKID 2: What do they do for fun? What do they do for fun?

THE BIRD: Hang out, play football.

SNIPES: Bruv do they have, butlers?

THE BIRD: No, some have cleaners.

SCHOOLKID 1: Do they all smoke weed? Do they all smoke weed?

SNIPES: Do they have yachts and that?

*"Do they all smoke weed" / "Do they have yachts and that"
continues as a musical round building to a climax until
interrupted by THE BIRD.*

THE BIRD: Yeah. Some do.

SCHOOLKID 1: Gosh.

SNIPES: Rah.

THE CAGE: WOW!

&&

THE BIRD: As time goes on, I like it more at Patrician Boys. People accept me, I accept them. The boy from the Badlands. With the occasional odd slang that others start to use, which I'm confused about at first.

Is this OK?

Does it work?

Posh white kids talking greeze and dirt.

And it was OK, in the end you know?

After a rapid ascension it reached a plateau,

SCHOOLKID 1: Whats up my n- /

THE BIRD: A LONG WAY BEFORE THE N WORD!

SCHOOLKID 1: -number one guy.

THE BIRD: Fam is as far as it gets.

SCHOOLKID 2: Safe fam.

THE BIRD: Calm.

The truth is the more time I spend,

The more I like these gents.

They are good peoples,

Just like my peoples,

On the other side of the fence.

I am the fall line navigating the hard and the soft, making sure that nobody rocks the boat too much on either side.

They are both,

They are all,

My guys.

Innit.

&&

TRACK SEVEN – FREE SPEECH

Chorus
Innit
You choose to talk like that
Innit
Speak better than that

THE BIRD: The lesson of English.

MATHS TEACHER: Why do you talk like that? You lot. Your generation?

THE BIRD: This our Maths teacher.

MATHS TEACHER: This school is one of the best in the country. And you, young men, are supposed to be some of the brightest minds of your generation, yet you choose to talk like that.

"Innit".

What is "innit"?

Why would you choose to sound so stupid? It is recognised in wider society, that those who speak well are more intelligent. That is the way of the world. Those who speak well are held in higher regard. Therefore, by speaking the way that you are, you are choosing to be perceived as not only less intelligent, but also for people to take you less seriously. To view you as a joke. I can't stand it. Speak better. Stop talking rubbish. Utter nonsense.

THE BIRD laughs.

&&

MATHS TEACHER: Is something funny?

THE BIRD: No, sorry Ma'am.

MATHS TEACHER: If there is something funny, you should say and share the joke. After all you are one of the biggest perpetrators of that stupid "innit" talk.

Well?

Do you have anything to say?

THE BIRD: I just think you shouldn't judge yourself by anyone else's standards. If you ask me that's stupid, innit.

MATHS TEACHER: ARE YOU CALLING ME STUPID?

THE BIRD: Detention.

&&

THE BIRD: Detention is fine

Just a waste of time,

But I guess that's the point. Waste peoples time. Prepare them for the future. Their future. Detention is just like training for prison.

Still it's another place to sit and to think. Between that and the bus that's all I do. Did you know the life expectancy of people who live along the same bus route can change by as much as five years? You can live one hour away from somebody and they are expected to live five years longer than you.

&&

I know you don't see what I see,
You don't understand what I speak
Our eyes see things differently,

I know what my version is
But to you my facts are alternative
We in the same place at the same time
But two worlds.
Politics.

31

THE CAGE: The lesson of Science

THE BIRD:

Through the process, of osmosis, I grow.
It's a fact, opposites attract
N these rich white boys love this broke black yute,
But naturally the opposite is true,
Of course, there's no way to force it
But I have to admit that I kinda love them too,
We were formed of many different elements,
But when we come together its not relevant,
Down to our very DNA,
We are different in every way,
But when you combine all the things in this,
You got a perfect synthesis,
Of the best parts of the whole,
From the suburbs to the road,
And so this bird has to evolve,
And become something new to behold.

TRACK EIGHT – ZERO CHILL

Chorus
Twelve years old and making a mark.
Trees, leaves, chill in the park
Bushes, weed, still in the park.

THE BIRD: Year Eight now. Twelve years old and in the park.

SNIPES: I got it! I got it!

THE BIRD: Snipes is hyped. Just running around skinning teeth.

SNIPES: I got it, cuz!

SNIPES: A job. The job!

THE BIRD: Big things. That's a lot.

SNIPES: Supermarket. Zero hours, so I can work when I want.
And hear what, they want me there at nights, restocking.
I don't even have to chat to dead customers, nothing.
Turn up, restock, go home. Like a Badman.

THE BIRD: Dope man. Way to go.

SNIPES: Safe, cuz.

THE BIRD: But zero hours, though?

SNIPES: Yeah.

THE BIRD: Will you get enough work with that, you know,
type of contract?

SNIPES: It's a trial ting. Four hours a week and we go from
there / if I do good.

THE BIRD: / Four hours?

SNIPES: Yeah.

THE BIRD: Aite, hope it works out for you, sounds like it
should.

SNIPES: It's still a job though man.

THE BIRD: Yeah it's a / fantastic

SNIPES: / Whatever! My yut. I shouldn't have told you fam.

THE BIRD: What?

SNIPES: How you gonna try and dead my hype like that?

THE BIRD: Sorry, I was just reading about how you have to
be careful with some / zero hour contracts

SNIPES: / Nah fuck that. Think I ever would have reacted that
way. Patronising, not even trying to hear what I got to say.

Not everyone can get a scholarship my G and go to some bullshit rich boy school.

THE BIRD: I apologised. It's not that deep.

SNIPES: Apologised? Nah, Fuck your apology, cuz try take me for a fool.

Before you never would have acted like that. Chatted to man so Dut?

Your talk don't even sound the same. Bare stuck up.

You do you G,

Imma do me.

SNIPES goes to leave.

THE BIRD: Snipes!

SNIPES turns back to face THE BIRD.

SNIPES and THE BIRD hold each other's gaze.

TRACK NINE – CODE. SWITCH.

Chorus
Type.
Type.
Talk.
Type.

THE CAGE: The lesson of Computing & Statistics.

> *Type.*
> *Type.*
> *Talk.*
> *Type.*

THE BIRD: The beat of the keys as we sit in I.T. Messages flash on the screen as we

Type.
Type.
Talk.
Type.

On the computer. Teacher doesn't know. It's supposed to be banned this ability to send each other words,

But guess what? We hacked it, coz after all we are still nerds.

On my screen, it seems that people feel freer

As we

Type.
Type.
Talk.
Type.

My classmates all around me in the same room, in the same chatroom, in the same room.

But I don't know, who's saying what. Our names are in code. Just in case the teacher clocks of course. It's our last line of defence. Our firewall.

In computing there is no grey. There is only wrong and right, black and white.

Ones and zeros, binary code. YES or NO. True or False. And as we

Type
Type.
Talk.
Type.

In this room, in this room, I see that my classmates' views are the same. I can't even tell who's typing because I can't see their names, but the keyboard warriors are rising.

KEYBOARD WARRIOR 1: Black people should be stopped and searched more often because they commit more crimes. You can't complain that there is a problem with police when statistically the problem is with black people.

THE BIRD: Yes / but you can't…

KEYBOARD WARRIOR 1: / No buts. Ones and Zeros. Binary. We know, Stats show, it's because they are from broken homes, no fathers. No role models.

THE BIRD: *(Looking around the room and searches the audience.)* Who the hell is K5bomba, I know you are in here.

KEYBOARD WARRIOR 2: Yeah so that's why they lose their way, more easily lead into crime you see. Black guys are way more likely to go prison.

THE BIRD: Great now jamlover8 is jumping in. And as they

> *Type*
> *Type*
> *Talk.*
> *Type.*

I don't. I won't but I should, because what they are saying is wrong. Opinions and facts muddle together, and I need to correct their . . .

KEYBOARD WARRIOR 1: Binary. Yes or No. True or false. Black or white. No Grey.

And they can't get jobs, so of course, they will be led into more crime. It's not their fault, black people are naturally more violent, it's a biproduct of slavery.

THE BIRD: *(Looking round the room with increased annoyance.)* Nudgefudge82 you have done it. You have overloaded me with your input. I can't take the talking anymore so I must...

Type.
No.
This is wrong.

KEYBOARD WARRIOR 2: No?

THE BIRD: No.

KEYBOARD WARRIOR 2: No, you are wrong. Binary. Yes or No. True or false. Black or white. No grey.

THE BIRD: No. No. No. My memories are more reliable than your facts.

Type.

My memories are alive and volatile, but they exist, you can't wipe them away with stats.

That you reboot repeatedly.

That you ram down my throat.

Somehow to me, being black overrides *reading* about being black.

There is nothing to teach me on my specialist subject, your information is biased from the fact,

You are white. You don't live this life.

...
...
...
Type.

KEYBOARD WARRIOR 1: No.

THE BIRD: No?

KEYBOARD WARRIOR 1: No. You can't argue with facts. It's there in black and white.

THE BIRD: No grey?

KEYBOARD WARRIOR 1: No way,

To contest what is factually correct.

And did you know black people are more likely to be mentally ill? That's also why they have more criminal behaviour because they inherit mental health problems...

THE BIRD: Luvaluvahuggabruva types.

> *And they type*
> *And they type.*
> *And they talk.*
> *And they type.*
> *And I stop.*

Because I know there's no point in writing, in typing, in this.

The outcome is already fixed. It's a closed loop.

But at least I spoke up a bit.

Maybe I changed . . .

Something.

KEYBOARD WARRIOR 1 & 2:

> *Bird,*
> *Before the person typing was that you?*
> *Sorry if I offended, didn't mean to be rude.*
> *And anyway, we all know you're not that type of black dude.*

Interlude

THE CAGE: THE LESSON OF FOOD & NUTRITION

THE CAGE hands out bottles of water/sweets.

TRACK TEN – THE PLEA

<u>Chorus</u>
Billin a zoot
Like always
Sat in the park
Like always

THE CAGE: Lesson number nine, Economics.

THE BIRD: Year Nine hits. I'm thirteen now. I'm doing better. Kind of. I still get a lot of detentions. I'm sure I'm on track for the school record but puberty has helped. I haven't calmed down, but other people are now more of a problem, so I don't stand out as much. And I now fully get why every grammar school is same sex because puberty makes girls, boi, a problem. At the very least a distraction. At the worst you are failing your GCSEs. I still go to the park, I don't have a house key and my mum works late but to be honest, these days I spend more time in the library. It's better, more to do. Today is a park day, but I'm late. Detention.

Snipes is seventeen and still here.

SNIPES: Like always.

THE BIRD: He is billin a zoot.

SNIPES: Like always.

SNIPES: Detention again fam? Fucking hell, what for this time? Running your mouth off again, I bet. You need to learn to be humble and shut the fuck up. (*Laughs.*) You never learn man. But listen though, I wanted to ask you something, on a real. You know them people at your school, some of them got money, right? You told me before some of them are balling, so I'm guessing like one two of them must have some hook ups. Like their parents own a business something or they got links to somebody who can hook a nigga up or something. I need a job fam. For real. Money is tight, had bailiffs knocking on my mumzy's door today cuzzy. For real. Had me ducking down and hiding and shit and even though I'm doing the legit thing, I'm not making enough man. Supermarket ain't cutting it. I was late a couple times and then they started cutting my hours down, and I lost my head a bit fam, you know dem ones dere, I lose my head sometimes cuz, I know its dumb, but I can't help it. Now I can't even find a shift and I can't see no jobs that I will make serious P, so I'm asking cuz, like I'm asking you to hook a nigga up, if you can. Please. These streets are dirty, every single time I take my eyes off the streets to look to the sky, to look at the stars, I run into some shit. I need a way that's not round here man, I need a way out. Will you ask for me, yeah?

THE BIRD: I know some of my friends from school do have parents with businesses. Some of them have good jobs. And I know that maybe if I asked around somebody might know of a job, somewhere. But I also know that they wouldn't employ Snipes. Not in a million years. If they had a chance, an opportunity it would be for someone else. And I don't know, how I know that without asking, but I just do. And I don't know how to tell him that.

So, I just nod.

TRACK ELEVEN – FIRST. CONTACT.

THE CAGE: Lesson number eleven, Languages.

> *Together were two cages hung,*
> *For music and for show;*
> *In one a fine canary sung,*
> *In t'other screech'd a crow.*

THE BIRD: There are two trees in the same garden. The garden
is massive, and the trees are far away from each other, on
opposite sides. In one tree the canaries live, singing their
song all day and the other tree, is the home of the crows.
The crows screech to talk to each other and are loud and
brash. They both live in the same garden, but they never
talk to each other, never interact, until one day a crow
decides to travel to the home of the canaries. The journey
is quite hard, but the crow is determined. The crow wants
to make friends. When the crow makes it to the canaries'
tree he tries to talk them but he is too loud, too brash. The
crow is bigger than all the canaries and his screech
frightens them, so they run and hide.

THE CAGE:

> *One charm'd the household with his song,*
> *The other vex'd it with his cries;*

THE BIRD: The crow realises his voice is scary to the
canaries, so he tries to soften it. He has heard the
canaries' song before, so the crow tries to imitate it. For
two days and two nights the crow tries tirelessly to sing
the canary's song but it doesn't work. The canaries still
hide and so the crow gives up and flies back to his tree.
When he gets back the crow tries to talk to his family and
friends, but his voice has changed. His screech had
become weak and dainty through the effort of trying to
sing the canary's song and nobody can understand him.

The crows throw him off the tree, scared of the thing he has become.

The crow flies to the middle of the garden between two trees.

An outcast to both, he has no home.

There he dies.

TRACK TWELVE – BANG. FLIP. REVERSE

Chorus
Don't try nothing
You won't get hurt
Don't try nothing
And don't fucking watch me

THE BIRD: The hardest lesson. P.E.

SNIPES: GIVE ME YOUR FUCKING PHONE! What else you got, you got money? Don't try nothing, as long as you don't try nothing, you won't get hurt, do you see it? Do you understand? Empty your pockets, I don't want your sim card, I'm a nice guy, you can keep your sim card, you can keep all you contacts and that, just give me your phone. What you looking at? Don't watch me so hard. Hurry the fuck up!

I said don't fucking watch me. You got any money? GIVE ME YOUR FUCKING MONEY.

Simulated punch.

That's what you get for watching me!

SNIPES smiles and winks.

Yo!

SNIPES runs off.

THE BIRD runs off.

THE BIRD runs around the stage frantically until coming to a stop, back in front of the audience, breathing heavily. The letter drops, THE BIRD steps out of the madness.

&&

THE BIRD: He smiled at me. He winked. It was at a normal Wednesday. Finish school, four of us coming back and we are walking down the alley to the bus stop and I see Snipes and I'm about to call his name, but I just feel I shouldn't. If anyone has ever been around a situation where you know something bad is about to happen, there's a weight. It's heavy and dark and it fills the air like smoke and somehow, I knew s*omething* was going to happen. They didn't. Richard, James, Alex. It's like they weren't aware, they didn't pick up on it until it was too late, until he was there in their faces telling them to take out their money. But he didn't ask me. And I wanted to say, "Snipes my brudda, what the fuck are you doing", but I knew I couldn't. And then before I knew it, Snipes punches Richard and he hits the floor, bleeding. But before Snipes ran he smiled at me, said Yo! He didn't take anything from me, he didn't rob me, but he robbed my friends and I was so fucking vex, my heart was beating so fast watching this nigger, my nigger, this fucking nigger run away. I am shaking. My friends are shaking as well. They are shaking from fear and a little anger. I am shaking from a lot of anger and maybe a little fear. I try to make my shaking the same as theirs. I was so much in a daze I didn't realise they were shouting at me.

&&

JAMES: What are you doing? You got your phone still, he didn't take it, call someone! Call the police, call the police! Call the ambulance. Richard's bleeding, we need an ambulance.

43

THE BIRD: The question of what.

ALEX: What can we do? He's bleeding, what do we do? What just happened, What the hell is going on?

THE BIRD: The second wave of questions comes and that's the question of why.

JAMES: Why didn't he rob you alone?

THE BIRD: I don't know.

ALEX: Why have you still got your phone?

THE BIRD: I don't know.

JAMES: Why did he smile at you? / Why did he wink?

THE BIRD: / I don't know, I don't know.

Then the third wave comes too fast for me to dodge, like a close-range bullet.

ALEX: Do you know him?

THE BIRD: I don't know, I mean no.

JAMES: What do you mean you don't know? You either do / or you don't?

THE BIRD: / I said no, I mean I'm not sure.

ALEX: Do you know him or not?

Pause.

Silence.

THE BIRD: I don't know.

TRACK THIRTEEN – GET TOUCHED.

<u>*Chorus*</u>
Extreme circumstances bring extreme reactions
Extreme circumstances bring extreme reactions

THE BIRD: The famous philosopher Big Narstie said once said:

> *Man thinks it's exciting but hear what I'm trying to say. Sitting in the passenger sit of the car and seeing things happen and being first hand knowing that's your life what's going to be ruined, cuz, it's a different ting. Ya smell me? Man whose doing stuff out here for fancy trainers, to buy Balenciagas and that cuz is different from the man who's tearing down road to go Iceland and make sure his mum's OK. Do you smell me cuz? Them two guys – the guy who wants to go Iceland and look after his mum, understand... he will drop you. The guy with the Balenciagas is going to talk because he don't really want to do it. Do you smell me fam?[1]*

Things aren't that simple. Sometimes them two people, the guy who will drop you and the guy who will talk

Are the same person

At a different time.

The only difference is desperation.

ALEX: Do you know him or not?

THE BIRD: Kind of, I mean, no.

When you see five guys walking down the street hooded up you don't know what their situations are. You don't know which one would be the one who would drop you and which one would be the one to run away, to help you,

---

[1] 'Big Narstie keeps it real about grime'
(YouTube: https://www.youtube.com/watch?v=kEwv8xOLUI0)

to cry. Most of the time they don't know themselves. Extreme circumstances bring extreme reactions.

JAMES: Do you know him?

THE BIRD: I don't know.

Most people are fortunate enough to go through life never having to confront a situation that forces them to confront the very depths of their soul. That forces them to ask the question; what am I truly capable of when I am pushed to my limits? How would I react?

ALEX: DO YOU KNOW HIM?

THE BIRD: I SAID I DON'T KNOW!

THE BIRD goes to punch THE CAGE and stops.

&&

TRACK FOURTEEN – R U MAD?

Chorus
Serious incident
If you know please call
Serious incident
If you know please call

THE CAGE: Lesson number fourteen, Sociology. Citizenship.

THE BIRD: Over the next few days they tell us that nobody is to travel by themselves. Everybody must be in small groups. Those yellow and blue signs go up. Serious incident, robbery if you know anything please call the police on… You've seen them, right? Everybody has. Or at least I thought they had until that week. The week when the signs went up. Everybody is stopping to look at them and read them, people are shocked. I see people standing around and shaking their heads, visibly affected by these

46

yellow and blue signs that I walk past every month. All the time in my area. Signs that say robbery, murder, stabbing whatever I just accept them as part of my reality at home and keep it moving, but these people from Patrician Boys are scared. Truly scared. And as I stand there watching them I realise they are right. The problem isn't with them, but with me. When you live in an environment, you become desensitised to it. It's not like I never thought those signs were bad, I just didn't care enough. I got used to them. After all, where I've grown up is fun. There are real friendships, real families, real love. The violence and the problems are things you never really pay attention to because it either doesn't affect you directly or you are focusing on the love that was all around, all the jokes. At Patrician Boys I once heard my school friend say that their whole family is waiting for their grandmother to die, so they could inherit her money. Now that shit is fucked up to me, but I guess to him, that is normal. The truth is everyone gets desensitised. Everyone gets used to what they get used to. Some people don't notice the violence, some people don't notice the love.

&&

SNIPES: I'm so sorry fam. For real. I didn't know you would be there. It was just bad luck. It was supposed to be a quick ting, first people I saw just get the P and out. And you said to me before these people got money, so I thought, fuck it, they won't miss some of it. Or a phone or whatever. I just needed some quick P. I didn't think anyone would get hurt. And I didn't think even for a second that the people that came would be you and your guys. I'm so sorry fam, I didn't mean to get you involved in my shit, believe me. I couldn't believe when I clocked it was you, but it was already too late. I had already started moving you man by the time I clocked it was you. How's that yout? I hope he's alright, for real. I had to drop that yout, I'm sorry fam he was getting brave. He was going to try something I saw it. I saw it in his eyes. He clocked there was four of you man. I saw him clock four of you, one of me. He was going to try a ting believe me. I'm sorry. If the police ask you something I beg you, say you don't know me. I beg. You known me since nursery times man. I always had your back, just do this one thing for me please fam. Please. I'm sorry.

THE CAGE:

> *One charm'd the household with his song,*
> *The other vex'd it with his cries;*
> *Forever cawing all day long,*
> *He call'd for bread, and cakes, and pies.*

TRACK FIFTEEN – THE GIFT OF THE CURSE

Chorus
Old men
White suits
Don't need an excuse

THE CAGE: Lesson number fifteen. Media Studies and Citizenship.

THE BIRD: There is nobody more racist than people from their own race. Nobody. Nobody hates blacks more than blacks. There is nobody more Islamophobic than Muslims. That's why it's jokes to me when there's an issue with a black gang, or a terrorist attack and you get this small window of opportunity where old white men in suits come out in the media, and it becomes socially acceptable for them to express their bigotry. I listen to what they say, and it's tame compared to what is said privately behind closed doors. Tame! Cah, people from minorities already know the level of bullshit they are going to have to deal with based on the actions of others. They already know the next time they open their door and walk down the street they may be subject to abuse from a stranger for something that has nothing to do with them. They already know they will be judged and must fight harder just to be considered "OK" in wider society. Just to fit in. So, they have hate in their heart just as much as the privileged people who find their voices in the media, probably far more. But it stays whispered behind closed doors because it *has* to. Because it must. Because when we open that door and step out, we have to be figures of dignity and peace. Stepping out angry just confirms what those old white men in suits want to think. You become an example in their narrative. And they sure as hell don't need any more of an excuse to be racist.

HEAD OF YEAR: There has been an accusation that there seemed to be familiarity between you and the assailant. All three other boys involved in the incident have said the same thing, to varying degrees. Yet, when asked you have denied this. This is a very serious incident, do you understand? This goes beyond the school, this goes beyond just you and me, this is a criminal police matter. Should you fail to comply with their investigation you could be facing a charge of obstructing justice yourself. And you could get a criminal record. For the sake of what? I'm telling you this because I like you. I am telling you this, because I care, and it hasn't gone far enough yet for it to affect you long-term. Should you help the police now anything you may or may not have said, any lies you may have told will be put down to youthful indiscretion. If you or your family have been threatened in any way, if you're afraid of this young man, the police *can* help you. They can protect you. I promise you, the young man who committed this crime has no future, but you do. And you are putting it in jeopardy for something that may seem important to you now, but long-term it will not. You have been doing much better here; there is even talk of you

becoming a prefect or a mentor to younger children
who might face similar problems. Come from similar
backgrounds. There are times in a person's life when they
must make important decisions. Usually they do not
happen for one so young, but I know you are capable of
understanding what is going on here. What implications it
could have. And I know that you can deal with it. This
moment is a crossroads for you. Ask yourself, what are
your ambitions, what are your aspirations. Who is the man
that you wish to become?

&&

THE BIRD: Ambitions. Aspirations. The man that I want to
become

Ambitions.

Ambition bothers me.

Ambition without opportunity is what kills people.

All I do is think.
Like when you wake up, with no cake up, roll downstairs to get fed
but you got nothing there, except hunger
and you get this stress on your head.
Certain man will accept that,
Never overstep that
Climb right back into bed.
But when you got a fire to do better that's when the problems start.
Ambitions and no options lead people places that are dark.
Movement, power, whips, garms.
All you see is things you should be reachin' but you can't see a path,
That's aspiration, pure motivation, without any chance.
Whips and garms, poppin bars, all bullshit and you know it,
But there's no way to control it.
When you got hunger, real hunger perspective gets out of hand.
How far you will go to progress, depends on the fire in your chest.

There ain't man, in a gang, banging man, without a plan to do
better.
Starts with ambition and ends in a Beretta.
Your ambition is, good grades – Uni – good job but there's
no ceiling. Nothing stopping, no block.
If you really got ambition and something's in the way of your
breaking through with a Glock.
Your idea of life is different like it or not.
Be a man,
What kinda man can I be.
Without heart for the things that made me be where I be.

HEAD OF YEAR: Do you know him? You can tell me.

TRACK SIXTEEN – BLESS

<u>Chorus</u>
Politeness, politeness like a brick wall
Politeness, politeness, after four days off school

THE CAGE: Lesson sixteen, R.E.

THE BIRD: Richard has been off school for a few days and
rumours are spreading. People are saying how he has a
broken nose and needed surgery to correct it. But the
operation went wrong, they messed up his new nose and
ruined his facial features and now he looks like the
Elephant Man. Or that the surgery went so well that he
now has a whole new face and looks like a supermodel.
Whole heap of madness. It's crazy how rumours can
spread though. Snipes has turned from a skinny
seventeen-year-old black kid, to a seven-foot hench black
guy. Still black though. When he tried to rob us, Richard
had bravely stood up to him and so he had been taken out
with a baseball bat. Don't know where the baseball bat
came from. The first swing had missed but when Richard
saw the bat was going to hit James, he jumped in the way

to protect him. And that was like with just four days off school. Richard has become a hero, whilst things with me on the other hand have fully gone back to day one. The day I got into a fight. The day I was other. Nobody is saying anything to me about it, but I know they are talking about me. There are stopped conversations when I walk into rooms, nobody wants to hang out without me outside of school and yet everyone is being polite. That's what makes it worse. The politeness. If people are being rude, at least you can address the situation, you can have it out with each other, work through the beef but politeness is like a brick wall. An obstacle of true friendship. Disabling and stagnant. But nice, so that's cool right?

&&

Today Richard's come back and everything changes. He's walked in, same Richard, same guy. With a slight black eye. We haven't spoken all day. He's been too busy with his new found fame and honestly, I've been avoiding him. Perhaps out of shame, I don't know if I can confront him. What would I say?

Anyway,

It's the end of the day.

Last period, last lesson,

We've all got to go home and they've implemented this "buddy" system for protection.

Everyone is avoiding my eye contact, trying to go with anybody but me.

But other.

And Richard just comes over to me straight. Bang.

RICHARD: You want to travel with me man?

THE BIRD: And I'm like

Sure. I'd love to.

I'm Polite.

So here we are walking, and it's fine, it's all good, we are catching jokes, it's like old times, but as we are walking, I know where we are heading and that is doing my head in, because I know that on this journey we are going to have to pass a destination that I don't want to face. That I'm not ready to see. That alley. That valley. With the shadows of death, from when Richard got punched, fell, hit his head and I truly didn't know, when the blood started to flow, if he would make it. Jesus, when the blood started to flow and the feeling of sin started to grow, deep within my soul, even though, I didn't know, Snipes would be there. Snipes would do that. To me. To my friends, I still couldn't cleanse, the feeling of guilt. The feeling of regret. And now the shadows of the past are in the present, coming closer with every step.

But I don't let it show.

I'm polite.

And then there it is. And all I'm thinking is shit. A straight path that I cannot see the end of. A small well-lit alleyway fills me with a fear that I have never experienced in my life. I am afraid. But I know I cannot let it show because he is with me. By my side. Richard. I must swallow my pride, my fear, my self-loathing, my worry, my doubt and *smile*. Be strong and courageous and step . . . out . . . on . . . (have faith) to the path. We walk, we vibe, we laugh, but it feels a little different. Maybe it's just me.

Hopefully. It's just me.

Hopefully.

When we get to the same spot, he stops. The spot where it happened. The attack. And then my defences crack, and it's a flood. I can't smile. I can't be polite. All the feelings that I have bottled up come flooding into my chest, contradictory and confused with no clarity or reason. My cup runneth over, my head is a mess and if he turns to me right now and asks me for the truth. I will give it to him. I'll confess. All I know is I'm not going to lie. I couldn't lie to him. To Richard. To my friend. God give me strength.

&&

RICHARD: You know there's a lot of rumours going around school about you right now? People are saying you had something to do with the attack on me. People are saying that I shouldn't trust you, but I don't care. James came up to me today and said that everyone in the class was planning to ignore you from now on, in my name, and I told him to shut up. I know you had nothing to do with what happened here. I was unsure at first but, I spoke to my Dad about it. About that boy. About when he said something to you. My Dad said to me that as Christians, we must follow our hearts and let faith lead us. That's when I realised that you are my friend and I have faith in *you*. Don't worry, if I hear any more of those bullshit rumours I will shut them down. Nobody knows this but that wasn't the first time I have been mugged. It was the third. I know people only think you are involved because you are black, but every time I had been mugged it has been by black guys and believe me you are nothing like them. They are scum, you are not. Maybe when we first started school, I would have thought it could have had something to do with you but you've changed so much. Getting to know you has been wicked and you're somebody I'd like to be friends with forever. Anyway, I just want you to know you don't have to be nervous or anything around me, I trust you man. We're cool.

THE BIRD: Rah. Ted.

TRACK SEVENTEEN – BREAK THE CAGE

THE CAGE: The lesson of Music

THE BIRD: A canary and a crow are having a heated argument. The canary is saying that its voice is better, and people like its song more. The crow is saying that it sings better, and people like its song more. This argument goes on for hours until finally the canary says…

THE CANARY: Right, boom lets settle this thing. No matter how much we argue we will never agree and it's getting long so hear what, the next creature that walks past this tree, let them decide. We will both sing to them and whichever one they choose, is the winner, ya get me?

THE BIRD: The crow thinks about this for a minute and then agrees.

(Under breath.) 'DONE!'

Wastecadetthinkingyoucansingbetterthanmewatchimgonna destoyyounappyheadedfoolcomingupinmytreewithyour deadsongthinkingyoucantellmesomethingluckyIdontboxya downonetime.

The canary and the crow go back to their perches and wait whilst glaring at each other. They wait and wait and eventually a pig trots past.

THE BIRD enters as the pig

THE CANARY: Pardon me, might you do me the honour of observing a little wager between my friend and me? We both believe that we have the better song and cannot decide, might you take a listen and offer your opinion?

THE BIRD: The pig nods in agreement and then sits down. The canary and the crow go at it. Playing the best song, making the best sound that they possibly can, and the pig says nothing; just stays seated, eyes closed, ears pricked. The pig listens intently to every note, every cadence. He doesn't miss a beat. Then after a very long time he slowly rises to his feet.

The pig looks between the two and then simply says,

The winner is the crow.

Then turns and leaves.

The pig leaves. THE BIRD returns.

The canary stands speechless. Then tears start welling up and turn into a sob. Which turn into cry. Which turn into a wail.

THE CANARY: How could I lose. How could I fail?

THE BIRD: The crow spreads its wings and asks what the problem is? After all it was the canary who set the rules and the pig decided, they should just move on.

THE CANARY: I'm not crying because I lost, but just look at my judge.

Silence

THE BIRD: That's where the fable ends, and you're supposed to take away from that; I don't know.

I imagine the canary coming down from his tree and confronting the pig.

THE BIRD leaves. The pig returns.

THE CANARY: Pig, why didn't you choose me? You know I've got a better voice, you know that I sing so much sweeter.

THE BIRD: Yes, canary I agree you do have a nicer voice. Any other creature in this forest would have chosen you. But the question you asked me was who had the better song. And even though you do sing well, your song doesn't speak to me, doesn't speak to my experiences nor what I like. To me the crow's song hits harder, resonates with my soul. It's more real. When I hear the crow's voice I hear struggle, I hear pain and I relate to that completely. I relate to the judgement and prejudice he has experienced in his braying cries. Your song was just fanciful nothings, and I found it soulless.

&&

Then the pig drops the mike and the crowd go wild.

THE CAGE: The crowd goes wild.

THE BIRD & THE CAGE: The crowd goes wild.

&&

The music builds whilst THE BIRD and THE CAGE dance around. Getting increasingly involved in the song. In the music. It should feel as though they've lost themselves completely and utterly in the music.

THE ACTOR:

Boom. That's it. Play's done. Or it was, but people keep getting in my ear. What happened to the bird? What happened to Snipes? So, imma let you know.

The same thing happened to both.

Both realised that they couldn't survive in their nests. So, both of them went right to the edge. And jumped. And they both flew.

And that brings me to my last lesson. Anybody know what it is? Shout it out.

THE BIRD takes suggestions from the audience as to what the last lesson is or could be. "Drama". "Dance". They are both part of it. The guesses continue until finally we get to art.

THE BIRD: That's it. This is it. This is my lesson. This is my art.

I dare you to try and tell me it's not relevant.

THE BIRD and THE CAGE leave the stage any way they want to.

End.

Printed in the USA
CPSIA information can be obtained
at www.ICGtesting.com
LVHW020944171024
794056LV00003B/953